What We Call Home

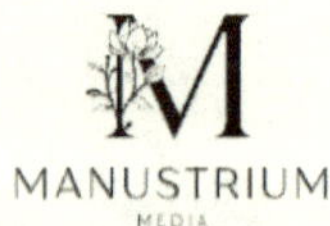

Manustrium Media
848 S Indianapolis Ave
Tulsa OK 74112

ISBN
Paperback 979-8-9859486-8-4
Ebook 979-8-9859486-9-1

LCCN 2025911333

Editor | Jes McCutchen
Cover Art | Sapira Cheuk
Cover Design | Jes McCutchen
Formatting | Racheal Daodu

Contents

Introduction

When I first began conceiving of this anthology it was driving north on Yale at the stoplight where Big Splash is and my grandmother and I were talking and I suggested she could maybe see a counselor at her church for her grief and she laughed and said firmly, "Oh no, that's okay. I'm too old to be depressed. I'm just sad."

While I stayed at her house with her, I finished the first poetry anthology I edited, "Between the Mess and Magic." It was messy and she was proud. We did puzzles and I fussed over the layout and the order and the acknowledgements. And she was proud and gave me money to pay for a cellist to be at the opening. Because parents should be able to enjoy beautiful things, and live music is lovely.

She didn't make it to the release party of that anthology, but her spirit echoes ceaselessly throughout this one.

A confused and tired housewife. Married young and whisked away from the life she knew. One time she and I drove past the home of the other boy who wanted to marry her. But we didn't knock on the door. After being separated during the a war, he came home and moved her thousands of miles from family. Hoping for a child. Putting on airs and pretending to be rich. A pill or two to help the pain. The best grandma that ever lived. Worried about her kids all the time. Put herself in the way of her husband and her kids. Allowed him grace to be a good grandpa later because people can change and soften. Always knew she could be a teacher.

Always tipped well. Always laughed faster than most people gave her credit for. Just a little girl from Jersey is all she was. Far from home and doing her best. She was really good at puzzles. Until she wasn't.

The first time she showed me her mastectomy scars, I showed her my first tattoo and we ate goat cheese and drank beer out of glasses at an oil man's event and it wasn't as fun as too much lemon cello and a green penguin but we made do.

When I started to brainstorm what this anthology would look like I landed on "homemaking horror" as the simplest way to describe it.

I stand by that nomenclature, though I often add the caveat "ish" to the descriptor, to soften the blow that what some people perceive to be horror might not be what others do.

I had postpartum anxiety and depression. I still fight intrusive thoughts. To me, doing dishes at a kitchen sink can take on the tension and apprehension and worry of horror. Or it can just be dishes.

Holding a tiny baby infant is the most beautiful thing to experience running parallel to all the worst thoughts of what could possibly go so horrible and irrevocably wrong.

The fear of losing what we hold closest, what we call home, can rattle around in our heads and ricochet off the dust boards.

Thank you for reading and supporting indie authors and small presses,

Jes

Notes on the imagery

All of the images throughout this text are by M. Torres. The titles of the images are taken from poems throughout the collection, and once again her art has so beautifully pulled together a collection I've edited. I don't know how she does it, but I'm so grateful for her.

Notes on the text

While many of these stories and poems are purely fiction, some are not. I think everyone can find parts of themselves in these pages, but if you do and it's too much, I have included a list of local (to Tulsa) and National (US) resources.

This collection explores many difficult topics including, but not limited to:

Sexual assault - Traumatic Birth - Rape - Gaslighting - Blood - Body Horror - Fire - Domestic - Abuse - Grief - Mental Illness - Physical Abuse - Toxic relationship

If you have any specific concerns or questions prior to reading, please reach out to the editor, Jes McCutchen at jesmccutchen@gmail.com.

If you or anyone you know needs help please reach out. Listed below are a few resources that are available.

Tulsa Area:
Take Control Initiative (birth control)
Text: (539)302-3615

DVIS (Domestic Violence Intervention Services)
dvis.org 918.743.5763

US Wide:
Aid Access (reproductive health)
https://aidaccess.org/en/

National Domestic Violence Hotline
thehotline.org Text START to 88788

RAINN (National Sexuall Assault Hotline)
rainn.org (800)656-HOPE

Take care of yourselves and each other. We're all we've got.
-Jes

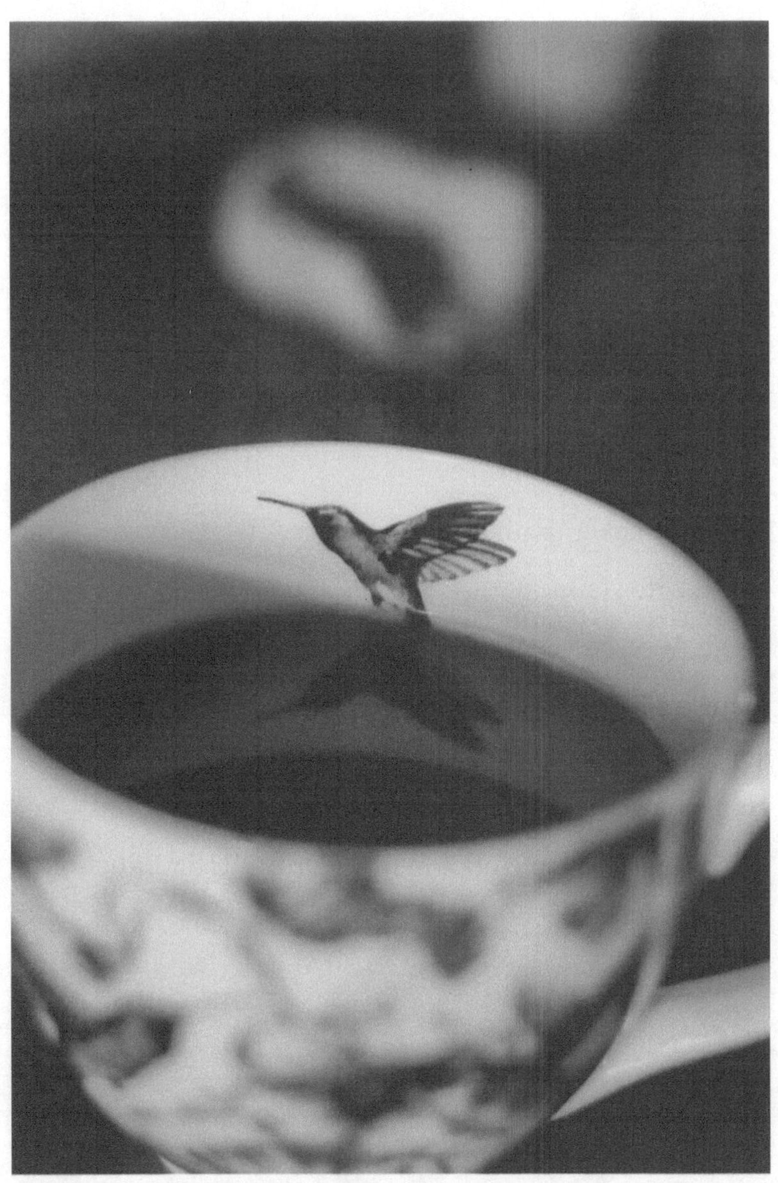

She is Our Lady of treading water

H.V. Patterson (she/her)

HomeUnmaker

with Kate Eleanor

smash
furniture pry up
floorboards frisbee
dishes out windows jump on
beds till frames
break muddy
sheets scrape
grout strip
paint hack
carpet tear
duster to bits with
your perfect smile unspool
pearls from
throat kick
off heels bathe
toes in grime.

and when you've unmade all you
loved, rendered home into gutted
house, pour
gas, strike
match, burn
what remains. Plant
a forest where your
past lived, breathe
free, your future
green

Housewife Haiku

a trapped fox
I gnaw at my wedding ring
but the gold snare holds fast

#

his hairs bristle in the carpet
she vacuums up the evidence
of his morning shave

#

his greasy fingers smudge
walls, windows, glasses
how much oil can ooze from one skin?

#

listening to true crime
while scrubbing the toilet
she discovers murder is easy

#

dinner will be ready when it's ready
eat your tongue
if you're so damn hungry

#

his muddy work boots sully
her pristine floor
she sharpens the axe

#

eyes widen
axe falls
the rest is violence

#

frozen blood coats the freezer
even dead
he makes a mess

#

sirens approach
I toast the flashing lights
with anniversary champagne

Saints Who Never Were: Our Lady of Homemaking

What makes a house a home?

Is it a hearth flame burning eternal
the kitchen alive with succulent,
roasting fat?
Is it a broom bristled with fallen hair
wielded against dust-deluge
of dead skin?

Home is where the heart is,
says everybody,
but so many hearts do not beat
where their bodies live and die

If you pray to Her:
She will offer neither salvation
nor deeper meaning
She is no bulwark
against depression's heavy hands

Her benediction, her fingers kissing brow,
will weather you
Her fingers laced with yours can only
callous blister burn

She is Our Lady of treading water
in the middle of the ocean
of feeding the serpent its own
eternal tail
She is the maintenance behaviors
we cannot divorce

Your grandmother worshipped Her with bruises
hidden under makeup
as she folded newborn father's clothes
Where is grandmother now?
Dead and gone

How do you honor Her
without losing yourself?
How, when you are a tide
subject to the Moon's gravitational pull which waxes
and wanes
but never ends

You cannot escape your own loss,
She croons, cratered face smiling
You cannot escape your erosion,
She wrecks your knees and compresses
your spine

She is a horror writ small
Saint of piecemeal loss
not Joan on the battlefield
but a martyr to drudgery and its killing-by-inches

And yet
there is savor in small breakings,
in tallying cumulative losses
dishes eaten and forgotten
floors cleaned and dirtied again

The Moon was once a Goddess
She could be again
if we let our hearts beat beneath Her cold skin
if we dared worship ourselves
reflected in Her

Crimson Colored Glasses

with Kate Eleanor

I've washed the dishes
vacuumed with teeth clamped tight
around a scream
struggled to dust blinds and baseboards
washedthedisheswashedthedishes
work must be done regardless
of griefs—now
I treat it as a meditation
a quiet defiance of entropy
my body cleans
serene automaton while I
daydream sweetly of blood

To Kanae Minato: Home Economics Teacher, Homemaker, and "the queen of *iyamisu*"

When you stood before your students,
their young faces weighed down by cram school—
Was that when it started?

Did you look at those pupils,
growing younger every year,
and see their egg-jelly fragility,
easily scrambled by unkind hands?

At home, as your fingers repeated
the patterns you'd taught,
the background noise of homemaking—
Was that when it started?

In the orderly prison of the classroom-home
you were an egg incubating
all the darkness you'd absorbed.

How often, in such banal and terrible ways,
do we fail the children
do we blame the children for the ways
the world cracks them open
and spills them out—
Are they guilty of our crimes?

Now, you are your ink-stained stories
the unthinkable—thought
the unsayable—said.

Show me, Queen of Iyamisu,
the predatory shadows
dressed in suits of flesh.
Show me the quotidian nightmares chasing
our children.
Show me my own shadowed insides
splayed on the kitchen counter
beside the bubbling pot.

Show me the truth:
there is no cleaning, no cooking,
no final absolution
that will scrub the guilt
from my unstained hands.

Will Anyone Even Notice When I Drown?

There's a monster in the basement.

I've tried to trap it, chase it away—kill it. But there's nothing to be done.

At night, it creeps up the stairs. It's made of dirty clothes, garbage tossed on the floor, pots and pans left overnight to "soak" in the sink, unopened mail, and water-damaged books. I hear it prowling the halls, though I am never fast enough to catch it.

It slides stealthily from room to room, licking inground dirt from corners, snorting dust from baseboards, snarfing crumbs lost beneath furniture, pouncing on anything out of place or abandoned on the floor.

No one else senses the monster.

My husband reminds me: we don't even have a basement.

But I feel it blundering through the house, this thing swollen from my homemaking sins, my slatternly ways. It gloats over my unwashed floors, my unfolded clothes, my unpolished silver.

Someday, I will start awake in the night. Beneath the comforting tempo of my husband's snores, I'll hear the door to our bedroom click open. He will not wake. I'll open my eyes, and the monster will be there, looming over me, an ocean of my failures, eager to collapse on the shore of my self-recrimination.

The next day, no one will notice that it's no longer me peering out through my eyes.

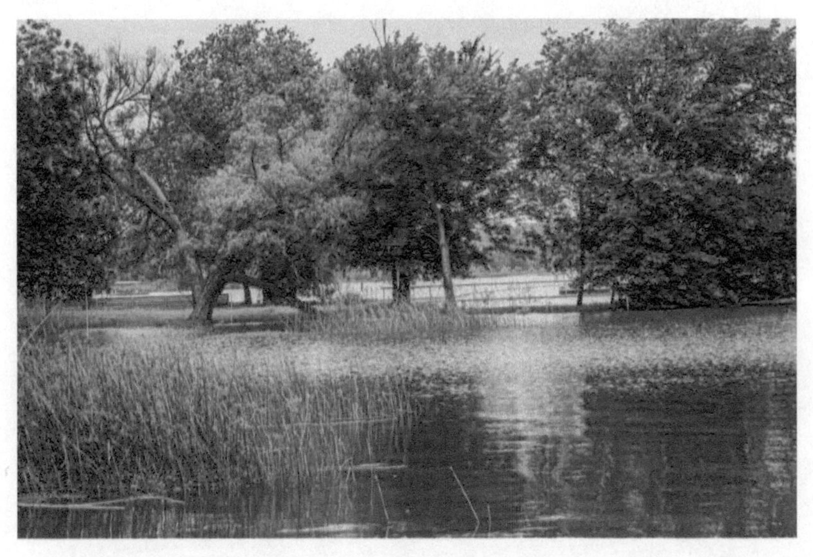

Some say there is a cleansing in the flame

Mariah Gonzales (she/they)

Mary Mother of the Motherless

When I die, I will go back to my childhood home,
11 Bass Drive, Sandy Park Estates.
My mother will be waiting angrily by the door,
asking why my brother and I are covered in bloody dirt
and dirty blood.
Bike crashes and four-wheeler wipeouts
were a part of our summer routine.
That was back when pain was just pain
and not a punishment I dole out to myself
when the guilt is overwhelming.
Mom never understood how we were still laughing
when she cleaned out our wounds,
ignoring the sting of alcohol wipes and Neosporin.
"It'll hurt for just a second," a hopeful promise I never
believed.
Even back then, I remember seeing blood
left me with a nostalgic feeling.
Maybe I was a vampire, a phlebotomist,
a serial killer in a past life.
I feel like that would explain a lot, unfortunately.
She called us lunatics when we brought home
the body of our favorite stray dog
to give him a proper burial.
Now, without anyone to scold me
for clinging to dead, decaying, decomposing things,
I become...
Necromancer.
That isn't the right word,

but it's the first word that comes to mind.
Screaming, "Breathe, breathe, damnit!"
while giving CPR to the useless lungs enshrined
within the corpses of my rotting relationships;
see also: dreams, past lives, even.
Mama didn't raise no bitch,
but she sure as hell did raise a deadlock
without a key,
a girl that leaves claw marks
on things that were never meant for her.

On My Knees

The fire I lost my childhood home to is still
burning within me.
I can feel the heat rising through my fingertips.
Sweat collects along my upper lip,
down my spine, like a fever.
The flames are burned into my retinas,
the stuffed animals with their eyes melted out of
their heads still follow me in my dreams.
I remember certain things,
like the clothes I wore to 5th grade,
that ended up becoming my only earthly
possessions.
I remember my mother laughing hysterically
as we walked through the rubble of what was once
our home,
claiming that if she didn't laugh, she would cry.
What little remains of my childhood photos
still smells of smoke, a decade and a half later.
Some say that there is cleansing in the flame,
I argue that instead, it fills you with the ashes of
everything you lost.

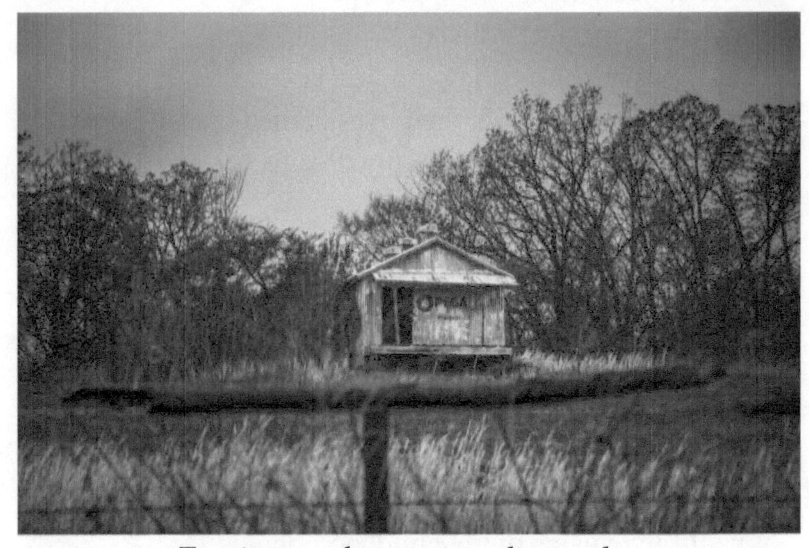

Turning my demons into diamonds

Juan De La Cruz (he/him)

What Awaits My Darling

I'm a fiancé now a title I thought I'd never hold,
and I'm going to be a father. Another title I thought
I'd never stand next to or have to call my own.

We're going to have a girl, and she will encompass
my world. But I at times worry about the world that
Awaits her, during her incubated slumber.

I am constantly, frantically grabbing pieces of a broken
world I remember to create a new one for my child to be.
But it seems… as determined as I am to build,

This world is intent on tearing itself apart.
My darling, what will you say when you hear the grown
ups
Talk about borders, and money while living people die?

I hope it's something cute, something to remind me,
There still good here; something that reminds me that
we can't all know those are shadows on that wall.

Not everyone knows indifference to ignorance.
It's like watching a rose bud fall and waiting for some
sympathetic sadness, but you know another bushell
soon comes.

"Ignorance is bliss"

My darling these words are so true,
that's why I don't know what I'm going to tell you
besides I love you; this much I know to be good
and true.

I can't keep the pain away from you, but I will be there to
explain,
I'll be there to help you understand that the pictures
are just shadows and when your ready

I'll
lead
you
out
of
the
cave.

And when I do I'll apologize like no one apologized to me;
for the truths we bury deep, grow trees that haunt us
while we sleep.

I don't know what this world has in store for you or who,
but I'll be here. The keeper of the gate, and holder of your
hand. Ready to bare my back so you don't have to brave

That I faced
Which alone.

I can’t create a new world, but maybe I can do something
while I'm here. So when you get older the world will be
ready
for you no matter how ready you are for it.

I hope as I pave the road others do the same, for what is
True may not be good but there are good truths all the
same.
Until then my darling,

I'll do my part, thinking, speaking, writing, waiting;
all about you, and the world that passes before my eyes,
standing at the ready for peace, or bliss.

Sorai's Sunrise

Now the train approaches. The ever
encroaching change is ever closer. And
I have to make peace that the front end
Of my life is almost over.

But what awaits is something beautiful,
Splendid, and a blessing. Your mother
And I await you like two candles in the
Night after months of necessary nesting.

The lights are low, and monitors beep as
We await your arrival. My queen rests
And I glance at the rainy blue morning
Threw Hillcrest's tin curtain slits.

What once was awaiting anxiously for this
day, now becomes eager anticipation to
Finally meet our baby, see her face, hear her
cry and feel her calm, enveloped in our warm
embrace.

One chapter ends, and another begins.
But this isn't just one chapter, you are a
new book, story and saga to be sure.
Though Your story is not yet written,

I
        see   thread
                        your   *sprawling*   past
                                                                                        Out   me.

Turning

Into lightning, striking.
No matter How frightening I ever once
thought before. What once was a question
Is now a single truth planted in my core.

There is sense, in the rise of fear, in the
dawn of a new life. It's because we site
our sun's dusk as their sun draws ever
near. One sun set’s.

And
on
The
other
end

We heed its rise.
Just as we hear our own names fade
into characters come and gone, in the
story of their lives.

And yet there is peace, for I know in you
Lies my hope for humanity. In you lies
All the sense I seek as a cure for my insanity.
Seeing that this is where it has all been heading.

All my life, my pain, my glory, my life's story,
were only the opening act for my bundle of joy.
Here I await your arrival realizing your heartbeat
is what has been missing; in this daunting life of noise.

D-A-D

For father's day I received a ring;
Made of gold and gifted to me
By the love of my life.

It was her father's ring.

D-A-D

gold crested across the top.
Three letters that carry the
Weight of the world.

Worn by a man with much life to live
But lacked time. Given to me by who
He cherished most and I

Realize his work goes
undone.

It was my *first* father's day gift.
A single sentimental token, with
three letters that tell me what's to come.

There are moments I can't help but
read the word. And in doing so
heed the meaning of it.

D-A-D

What does that mean to *me*?

The man I never met with the
Grand title on a hill distant?
What separates me from the rest?

And…

How do I give what I never got?
How do I be the man I never met?
How can I father but never knew dad?

D-A-D

A ghost in an adult's past.

That wrote today's trauma's or gave us
Warm memories that last generations.
Either way the memory retains love or pain.

I realize why all the great philosophers are old...

It's because that's when they had
all the answers.

D-A-D

As I read the band I
understand , you only know the trail is long
After you've walked it. Then can prepare

The ones on the way.

D-A-D

When the weight bares down on the shoulders,
And you can't help but feel alone even
When you're not.

D-A-D

When all you have is questions but it's YOU
that's supposed to have all the answers.
Even if you don't

D-A-D

I can't help but wander if my suegro (father in law)
Also looked at these letters and asked,
When did Atlas find comfort in his burden…

And finally see it as a blessing?

D
    A
        D

Who knew you could carry the
weight of the world on one finger,
In a single fathers day ring?

The Obligation

It is the curse of man,

to aim higher than
the ones that came before.
Sometimes it doesn't take much.

Be nice, think right say
what resides in your core.
Sometimes the bar is set so low

It must be PRIED
off of the floor.

So therefore…
We must do away with the curses
That linger in hearses

if we decide to be more.

Growing up with no dad
a lot of things were made harder.
Now it's up to me to see that those
things don't keep me from being
a good father.

Too many times babies suffer like cannon fodder.
Unresolved issues turn into used tissues,
And I don't want the same for my daughter.

This is my Mount Everest.

Reaching deep into the depths of my soul
For the sole purpose of becoming my best self.
Turning my demons into *diamonds*

Braving these raging raptures
of unresolved emotions
Because grown men can't be seen
threw the fog of Emotional explosions.

Only monsters in lonely hallways…

That is what awaits the father, who never bothered
To work on himself, FOR himself, or those
Around him.

My baby needs me, therefore I intend to be present.
Something one can't do if they harbor resentment.
For the man or men that never came threw,
for The broken promises, or ones
that were never made true.

So this is my promise,

I'll be there, first sunrise of a new day,
Till the sun sets and blue sky's fade away.
Until my sun sets, and the breath of my life
Turns to the wind that carries her beyond my heights.

I will be everything for her that I never had.
A shoulder to cry on, someone to rely on,
Or more importantly an actually present dad.
Because that's all little boys and girls actually deserve.

It's not the curse, but the obligation,
of men; to fly past the expectation ,
To strive and remember, we can be more
Than generational condemnation.

Life Lessons

There are times breathing isn't enough.
When mantras, and proverbs just aren't
Fighting that tough. When your tortured
soul tortures you back and all that's left is

The null,

And void.

Deep rested depressive episodes
Where I don't feel like myself.
Moments of pain, that I can't take
To anyone else.

What's worse is, the pain that's brought is
a new definition of what hurt is.
And sometimes I can see it coming at night
Bright like neon yellow; high viz.

Secret sleepers that show their peepers
When I'm at lowest like the grim reaper.
these intrusive thoughts make Me seem
Shallow but I know my soul is ten times deeper.

It's this sickness that afflicts me. Deep rooted problems
That if not acknowledged turn into sins like
Pride, gluttony, and envy. My biggest hope is
I do enough for my child, my biggest fear

Is that she'll be just like me.

Afraid to speak her mind, which leads
others to pass her by leaving her wondering
why can’t she speak more freely.
Its because daddy was always scared,
Told her not to do this or don't you dare.

Because
                That’s
                            What
Was
              Told
To him.

Just like his mom passed down things
that she held within. He stood his ground
ten toes down but when the time came
around the pain didn't stop with him.

So comes the time I make a choice,
When I decide that where the pain
resides It can be moved aside
So my future lineage can rejoice.

I can give the narrative change.
Because life is too short to let
Narrow visions guide your way in vain.
So as parents searching for our way
We must remember this isn't healing our pain.

It's your mother's pain,

Your mother's pain.

The people that couldn't love you
How they should've because they
Had their grip on too much rage.

Pain can be so dark

And yet

So

Trans - parent.

Which is exactly why we must turn these
Depressive impressions, into well learned life lessons.
The more we know, the more we heal our vessels.
And the better chance our kids have to pass on this
message.

Be yourself baby

Not your parents.

In the Plush Flower Tattered Blanket

I didn't know you could fit the whole
World in a plush flower tatted blanket.

That one day I could sing

He's got the whole world in his hands

And be talking about 8 pounds 12 oz 46
chromosomes of pure preciousness.

Sweet summer nights
Between two souls turns into
Dancing in your first apartment
Making dinner for the first time.

The very same apartment you'll realize
what it means to have a life partner,
Realize she's the one and eventually
Learn you're going to be a father.

Nine months you plot, stress and
reminisce. you'll plan, you'll fear; you'll
realize yesterday She told me, and
next week she'll be here.

One rushed trip to the hospital in the
dead of night turns into two phone calls,
three room changes And eventually
11 hours of labor.

Now holding the whole world in a
Plush flower tattered blanket. I can't help
But wonder where did the time go?
And where will it take us?

How will we teach her Spanish if we
Mostly speak English? Are we gonna
Go plum through terrible twos or
Will it go slow like midnight news?

She needs to be baptized, but what faith?
because I haven't yet had the
Chance to truly decide where my
Own soul will eventually reside.

I still haven't gotten over that when
She gets older I'll be responsible for
Selling my version of what I believe
Makes a good person.

Please oh please let's not talk about dating
To even consider that will take me years
Of mental rearranging. Put that next to noticing
How fast were all aging.

Every second that passes is another brick
In the home I'm building.
Everyday I wonder
how will we make her life fulfilling?

So many paths, and styles of parenting.
And at the same time we have to make sure
Our own damage is already done mending.

There's so much
                    Life
                              To live.

And your never sure how much time
You have to live it.

So I guess
          It’s *best*

That I take my time,
taking in my world

In the plush flower tattered blanket.

From Scratch

Have you ever had nothing
to eat in the house?
When I was younger my mom
 always found a way
So I had food to put in my mouth.

She would hit the kitchen
and you could see her gears fuming.
Just like when I get to my pen and paper
and wait for the muses to start musing.

She would dig through the cabinets and fridge,
Looking for anything, even a smidge.
Anything was enough.
She'd work with a speck, a morsel or a crumb.
She

Always

Made sure

I ate.

Because she knows how to make
something out of nothing.
She had to because she couldn't bare
to hear my stomach grumbling.

So here I am

Mumbling

Till I see it.

A few sentences scrambling,
a swarm of emotions and words
Rambling through the field of my mind
Like I'm knee deep in supper time.

The weight on my shoulders,
Is nothing compared to the single mom
That moved boulders, so I went to school
With my blue folder.

Now here I am

A lot of years later, a few years older
Quire a bit taller and a whole lot bolder.

And

I

Realize

All the words

I should have told her.

"You did a great job mom,
I didn't even know we had this in the fridge.
I really don't think my eight year old brain
Could have thought of this."

It's really something,
How she could make
 something out of nothing.

I see that now as I'm standing in my kitchen,
Looking at my cabinets, looking at the oven
Thinking I have to come up with something.

So here I go

For the family

Working against
the spirit of gravity.

Some tomatoes of trauma, serranos of
self inflicted judgement,
some garlic to adjust the flavors because
it's always good to cut with.

We got noodles of nostalgia on the shelf
That's always good to have when I'm looking at myself.
I got rid of the sugar cane, cause I got tired of

Passing

The

Blame

to

someone else.

I didn't know this is what adulthood is
And I don't know how she did it
By herself with three kids.

So I asked her once.

"How'd you do it?"

She replied

'no one else is'

That is the cold yet warm, and honest truth.
And you can't help but be thankful for it.
Therefore I have no choice.

I have to keep going, keep cutting, keep priming,
Basing, lacing, tracing , mumbling, and busting.
Serving up plates to those who come to me hungry.

Because I'm the one who has the ball
and I can't risk fumbling.

So here I am

in my kitchen

mumbling.

Because I didn't know my *whole* life,

My mom was teaching me

How to make something out of nothing.

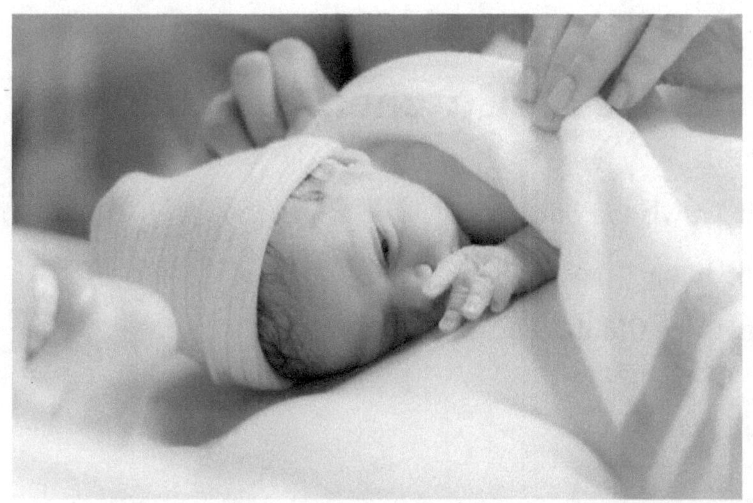

We can't all know those are shadows on that wall

Jes McCutchen (she/her)

It crawls to four

it crawls to four
time passing slithering
on the dusty floor
clawing one in forward
two feet back

i tug its hair
Nudge it forward
With my bare foot
Maybe break the hands
Of the clock
Just the short one
Just a little

But four comes too late
And lasts forever
I've already stalled
In the stagnant
Trap of living room carpet

Too tired to blink
Buffering
And buffering
And buffering

Lets the Child Feed

Lets the child feed
From my breast
Because someone said
My own vaccinated body
Might work to fortify
His small ineligible body
In this unease
Uneasiness of who
Will question
The late weaning
But no one outside
Of these barred doors
Will see us
Will question
Lackluster potty training
Hard to share
Easy to shy
Confused about stairs
Doesn't wear shoes
Or socks
If he can help it
How to tell them
Pause
It's just a wave

We'll wean in the next
Round of calm
Or walk forever
Wearing holes in the carpet
With jaws around
Our ribs

A Bloom They Said

A bloom they said
She opens up her womb
And three months later
The second thoughts emerge
Grotesque growth deep
Within her core
Intrusive thorns and thoughts
Behind undone dishes
Always postpartum we claw
Hand soapy and raw
Choking on the after birth

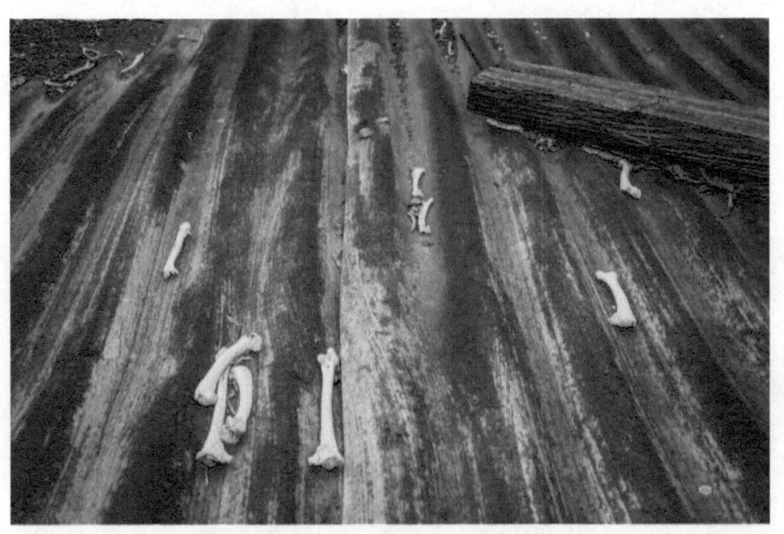

The second thoughts emerge

KJ Shepherd (he/him)

An Ephemeral Blip

To Sweep - Perchance to Sweep

Phases (with Jes McCutchen)

An Ephemeral Blip

Time is a bitch[1]. I woke up today and I was thirty-seven[2]. I could feel it. My back ached from the cramped way I was nestled betwixt the wall and my wife of fifteen years, Marjorie.

The dream I'd been having lingered in my head before churning into cosmic dust, leaving behind this... emptiness. This lack of caring. This ennui.

I couldn't attribute this feeling to anything concrete, so internally I blamed the dream[3].

I got up anyway, bones popping in protest as I went. Marj barely budged as I crept out of bed; beguiled by one of her own bewildering dreams, no doubt.

In the kitchen, I prepared my ritual sacrifice to the coffee gods, the aroma stoking the fires of wakefulness within. Then I went to make sure my little one was awake and getting ready for school. She wasn't.

"Hey," I said at her door while knocking. "Bus is here in thirty minutes, Stinker[4]. And you still gotta make your lunch."

There was a panicked creaking of her bunk bed as a response, followed by, "Okay! I'm up!"

I waited a few more moments, only leaving after I heard her stepping down the ladder and out of bed. The coffee was still dripping, so to pass the time I started some pushups. I'd been meaning to take my fitness more

---

[1] This has been long-confirmed and documented.

[2] Based on a true story.

[3] I really don't recall what it was even about now.

[4] A nickname, not her actual name. That would be dumb.

seriously, and today seemed as good as any to start. Had to shake myself out of this funk.

I was on twenty-seven when the dining room turned electric blue. I fell on my face, jamming my chin into the linoleum. *Damn!* I jumped up.

Two figures now occupied the space by my bookshelf in the living room. One was huge, easily eight feet tall, garbed in black robes[5], carrying a wicked sword that curved to the ground. His face was hidden in shadow, but I could *feel* him looking at me. My spine squirmed.

The other, much shorter figure was… me. Albeit dressed better; he had a fitted suit of classic black and white. And his beard was neatly trimmed, and less patchy; it connected along his jaw better than mine did. And he looked to be about thirty pounds lighter…

The robed figure waved his skeletal hand in a grand arc. "*This* is what you would have been." He was pointing at me.

I stood there, utterly without words, holding my chin, hair disheveled, garbed only in my SpongeBob pajama pants, where my gut sagged a bit over the elastic waist, sleep still crusting my eyes.

The other me spoke in a wail, his voice hoarse, "Please, oh great specter, spare me these twisted visions. I've learned my lesson! I'll change, whatever it takes!"[6] He collapsed to his knees and gripped the robes of the imposing figure, putting his full weight against the tall apparition, and yet it didn't budge an inch.

---

[5] See Appendix A for more information.

[6] Sound familiar? If you were thinking this sounds a lot like a line from "A Christmas Carol" by Charles Dickens, I had the same thought. Carry on.

The robed figure turned without moving, sliced a hole in the wall that bled pulsing blue light, and they both vanished into it.

The whole thing lasted only about ten seconds. A blip.

"What the fuck[7]!" I blurted out as the coffee continued to drip.

[7] I realize now how this might have sounded to my family, heard out of context. My wife, fortunately, slept through the entire affair. She still thinks I'm just regurgitating a particularly strange dream I'd had that night, and it's just bounced around in my skull so much that it's messed me up in the head. I mean, I'm not saying that it hasn't messed me up... My daughter though! She heard me yell "fuck" into an otherwise empty living room and still brings it up to this day.

Appendix A: The Tall Figure

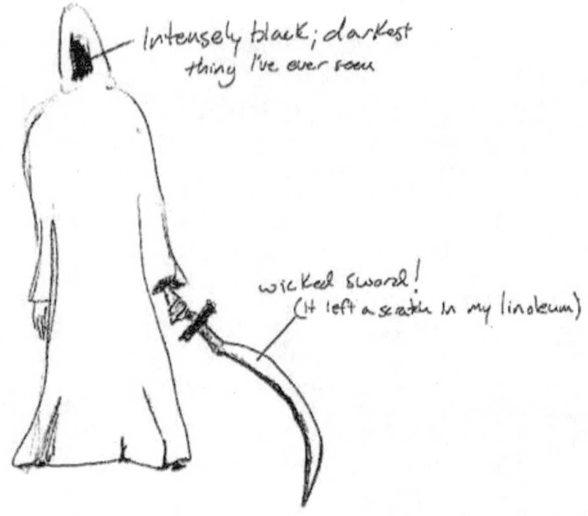

To Sweep - Perchance to Sweep

I sweep the floor, but filth remains,
A murky shroud, it stinks and stains.
My broom's a knife, it rends and scrapes,
Now grime from 'neath the floorboard 'scapes.

I scrub the marks as reams of dirt,
Old boards drink the past, scarred and hurt.
"You can have more, of course, my dear,"
The walls leak whispers, thick with fear.

The house is hungry, gaping wide,
It feeds on me; I cannot hide.
The ceiling slick with shadowed rot,
And every step a wretched thought.

I sweep and sweep, my fingers bleed,
The Filth, it laughs, my only need.
It never ends, this cursed task-
A living tomb, eternal ask.

Phases

Convinced it's a phase.
She can't be certain,
seen so little days,
much too young, too young

Projecting our own doubts
Onto their brave faces
Which must be a facade
I'm old. I'm older. I'm aging

Electing to trust
Clawing to trust
For I gain the most.
Preferential treatment than
My Absent counterpart
And myself?
this persistent boast

That you know better
another's true heart.

Puts on white gloves
And checks the hearth for dust

Released this daughter
of my mind, to find
Unearthed in the ashes
Unfrequented in love
The child of my heart

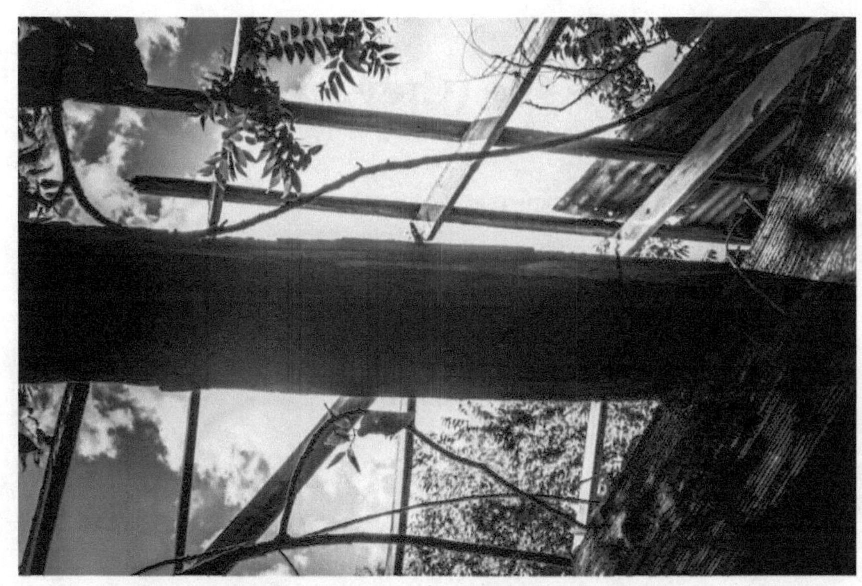

The walls leak whispers, thick with fear

Ashe (they/them)

Romancing a Gorgon

Romancing a Gorgon

an equinox ago
he stole into my lair
with cake
he soothed the beasts in my hair
with rotten honey

he said it was funny I walk so tall
said I was cute when I act so small
said he was sure I was worth the fall
cut a tail from my snakes
and then "missed my calls"

made me bleed
for the healing properties
within my veins
for the curve, the dips of my hips
the taste for blood on his lips

12 days ago
he asked me to drop my gaze and my ego
to find humility
he meant on my knees
he said he had a vision of me glowing, expecting

3 sunrises later
he said he “might” cum
like he said he “might” love me
as I performed the rites of the huntress
but he never confirmed either

2 moments later
the condom
lost to the abyss
and it was clear he did reach his zenith
the horror persists

8 days ago
I swallowed a pill
a plan
I didn’t really know about
until it was too late

5 days ago
I stopped sleeping
started dreaming of a nothing
she whispers
die

72 hours ago
he finally responded to me
offered to pay
“for my troubles”
I let him

yesterday I passed a black river
sludge
decay
too foul
I'm not okay I'm not okay I'm not okay

this morning
he broke contact with me
narcissistically
in a dark blaze of lies designed to isolate me from my community
meant to deny the disguise wearing thin

fucking men! never again.
because this weak version of me
didn't fit his perversion of me
and the coercion piece
wasn't working on me

the deplorable communication
his abdication
a speedy castration
if this is how he weaves his web through the trees
spitting around his male disease

so I built myself a castle
out of brass facts
a little Mt. Olympus
to try and shake this
need to speak

what a cheap relief
in playing weak
maybe if I had
gold coins in my mouth
instead of teeth

so when I speak
it filled the deep pockets
inside his head
maybe then
he'd of heard what I said about equal responsibility

line after line
of my heart
of my mind
an ancient story
his privilege to be ignorant

I dreamed I cut my tongue out
thats's what he wanted, isn't it?
through bloody bubbles
tried to spit
the echelon of my love

blood red
grotesque
unadulterated
too much
not ever enough

3 weeks from now
he's still inside me
his seed will still settle
in my gut
I'll want to tell someone

about the poppy blooming in my belly
about these sacred herbs
trying to root it out of me
but I won't be able to speak
with my tongue on the floor

I'll sit before my sea and wonder
what was all this for
what all this blood will grow
who else should know
the secret I keep

burrowed down deep
the furrow in my brow
my profound rage
that somehow I'm just supposed to move through
cause my silence suits you

but man, you have no idea what you don't know
that one look could have turned you to stone
that one song could have worn down your bones
made you beg
burn your own home

and even if you stop me speaking on this
I'll still resist, counter movement
a spell, a poem to Paul Monroe Owens
full legal name like a brick in his bed
to remind him it could have been his head

and I'd be justified
with the way this went
to send him
hell bent on subjugating me
to the gates of Hades

let you little simps work it out down there
fuck the patriarchy
And fuck that dude
this is why you're cancelled
men, you ruin the mood

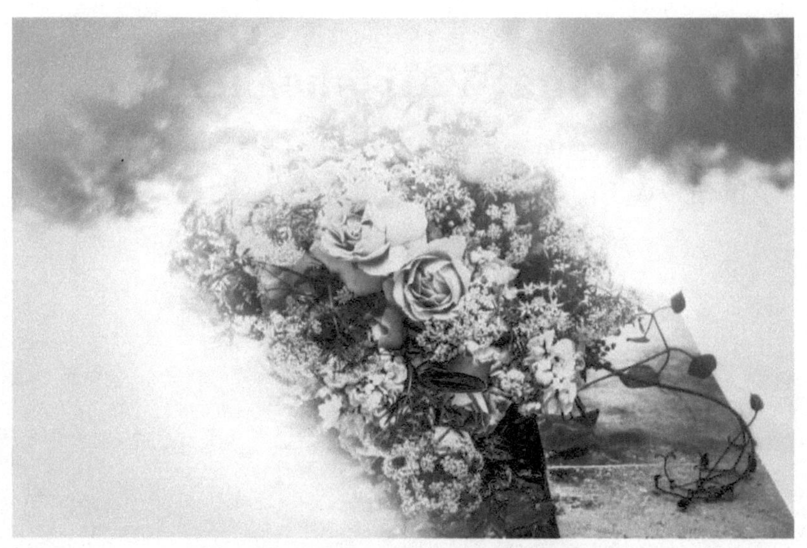

I'll sit before my sea and wonder

Tina Wall (she/her)

Alternative Uses for a Kitchen Knife

Alternative Uses for a Kitchen Knife

It started with loneliness. I was living with someone I'd moved to Austin for—someone I hadn't even meant to date. They didn't like to go out and be social, which was a huge change from the life I'd known—partying at gay clubs every night, before that at frat houses and college parties, and before that, staying out all night downtown, talking about literature like it meant something.

So there I was in the suburbs of Austin—bored out of my mind, bored of the person I was living with, and with maybe two friends. I had moved to Austin to try to stop spiraling—and instead, I spiraled in the opposite direction, just slower. This was early 2007, so I did what people did back then: I posted a personal ad on Craigslist. It was in the "Just Friends" section. I don't remember exactly what I said, but I know the title was "Zombies or Pirates"—again, very 2007. As a nerd in the early 00s, my friends and I had many debates on this subject, and me being a contrarian, I always said "Vikings." You responded with the same answer.

I think the first time we hung out, we went to see an incredible electronic band. Your taste? Impeccable. Of all the things that eventually went sideways, that one thing never wavered. You'd come by the video store and hang out while I closed, then we'd head to an all-night diner or the 24-hour coffee shop and talk about movies, books, music—everything. Eventually I was at your apartment until 4 a.m., introducing each other to the weirdest movies we could find. I'd broken up with the person I lived with, but I'd only moved into the spare room instead of moving out. So of course, that led to you and me making out.

You weren't just a red flag—you were the whole parade, and I ignored it. You were seeing someone else. I didn't care. We talked about past sex lives, and you told me—casually, like it was charming—about all the 16-year-old hostesses at your job at Bennigan's you'd slept with. You were 21. I still don't know why that didn't set off every alarm I had. My ex kicked me out after they did something deeply unethical and then got mad at me for reacting to it—so I went to your place. The first night we had sex—the first night I slept over—we were in that same filthy, maggot-filled studio I'd been to before, nothing clean, flies everywhere, in a rough part of town. Your mattress—on the floor, of course—was like an island in a sea of fast food trash and empty cigarette boxes. You had a particular fondness for Jack in the Box tacos. We woke up to an eviction notice on the door.

I lived out of my car for a couple of weeks while you moved in with your *actual* girlfriend. I stayed up for two days straight helping you move, only for you to leave most of it behind—except your computer, your mattress, and mountains of movies and dirty laundry. There were so many clothes, you kept discovering shirts you'd forgotten you owned. Then a friend—who I also kind of wanted to make out with—let me crash in her and her husband's living room. You became a frequent fixture there. We ended up having a foursome with her and her husband—technically separate but side by side. Then one morning, after you slept over, she woke up in a bad mood and kicked me out. I still don't really know why.

You were still living with your girlfriend, and I was living out of my car for a month this time. The video store had abruptly closed, so I couldn't even crash there overnight on close/open shifts like I sometimes had the last time I was homeless. I picked up a temp job with Apple when the first iPhone launched, doing metrics at the call center. We signed a lease for an apartment together, and I stayed with a friend for the month and a half until move-in. Somewhere in that month and a half—maybe a couple of weeks before move-in—you broke up with your girlfriend, and my friend let you stay at her place. She was honestly too generous. That's probably part of why she's still my friend.

About four days before we moved in to our new apartment, you proposed. I said yes, because I was an expert in denial. A week or so after we moved in, I got an anonymous email saying you were still regularly hooking up with your ex. I went home early so I'd be there when you got back, and I confronted you. You cried, admitted it, said you were really sorry or something—I don't even remember. Whatever you said, it worked. I forgave you. We put up with a lot of your ex's bullshit for a couple of months—police reports, calls to lawyers, nearly needing a restraining order—before she finally left us alone.

Meanwhile, I was trying to make a home out of our shitty apartment and plan a wedding. We were going to elope in Vegas, like my parents did. But your dad said he'd missed so much of your life growing up because of work travel, and he really wanted to be at your wedding—so we planned a small one in Austin, four days after Christmas, and saved Vegas for New Year's instead. As we settled into our so-called domestic life, you started doing little things I didn't yet recognize as controlling. It seemed like helpful suggestions: "Maybe don't talk to friends from back home if they make you homesick," "Unfriend people from college that you don't talk to anymore on Facebook." They sounded reasonable enough—so I did it without thinking critically. One little cut at a time.

You rarely made me come, and I never made you come. You had a bit of a humiliation kink and wanted me to say how small your dick was and how bad you were in bed—while you were inside me. I wasn't comfortable with that, so I just started giving you head a lot instead. You affectionately called me your blow job machine. I know now how awful and dehumanizing that was, but back then, I didn't. You constantly compared me to your high school girlfriend—stuff most people would keep to themselves, but not you. You genuinely couldn't get off without being humiliated, and I was starting to think you might have a porn addiction—not that I had a problem with porn, but you watched it constantly.

That fall, we both managed to wrangle customer service jobs at a video game company. The job was fun, but you were the one who actually made friends with our coworkers—not me. Our wedding was fucking depressing. None of my friends came, not that I had many, and I didn't even really have a maid of honor—I asked your best man's girlfriend to do it. She didn't do any of the usual maid of honor stuff that's supposed to help the bride. I handled everything on my own. A couple coworkers showed up, some of my family, and the friend who let us both stay with her—but mostly, it was your friends and family. We blew all the money people gave us as wedding presents on slots in Vegas.

We came back home, and tried to scrape by. Your parents gave you a Chevron gas card they paid off monthly, and we constantly ran it up buying food—because we couldn't afford groceries half the time. Canned food, jerky, and power bars from the neighborhood gas station was frequently our dinner. Oh and cigarettes. Somehow we were never without those. The barbs started getting sharper and sticking deeper not long after we got back. I often didn't want to have sex, because I knew you'd ask me to humiliate you. "I won't ask this time." So I'd say okay—only for you to inevitably ask. "Come on." "Please, Tina,

I'm so fucking horny." Over and over until you wore me down and I said okay just to shut you up. I now know that coercion, and demanding things that were explicitly discussed as a hard limit, are forms of rape. It's not enthusiastic consent, so it's not consent at all. I didn't know that then. I thought I was doing my best to be a good wife.

I got fired from our job for tardiness and missed days—the exact same number you had. But I'm a woman, so I got fired, and a month later, your contract was made permanent. I was furious. It felt like I was being discarded—easily replaced—and it hit me hard. I didn't just feel angry; I felt worthless. I didn't expect it, either. I'd assumed we'd either both be let go or both be kept.

I took a job at a call center, and started to make a couple of my own friends. One of them, Tim, eventually got me to come out to pub trivia with him and some friends—which, to this day, I still don't know why you agreed to. Maybe you were working that night and couldn't stop me. I was excited and surprised that I was being allowed to go socialize by myself. I made good friends there and started seeing them often. You seemed to like most of them once you met them—so I was allowed to keep seeing them.

Even Tim—because you two got along well. He'd made it very clear he hated when men made moves on married women; his former best friend had broken up his first marriage by having an affair with his wife. I was actually kind of jealous of your friendship with him. I was really protective of Tim, and I didn't want him to know how bad things were with my marriage.

Then your dad was in a horrific accident. I left work to meet your mom in the ER, and my bosses punished me by assigning me to the worst support line. I couldn't stand taking calls from that line all day, every day—not to mention, it took me off the UK shift I *loved.* So I decided to quit and be a housewife. *Hausfrau*, as we called it. For a while, it was mostly me trying to cook more and make sure your mom had whatever she needed while your dad was in the hospital. That included passing updates between family members, checking on her often, making sure she had everything she might possibly need, and sometimes even driving over two hours to and from their home to pick up things for her or for your little sisters. Your dad was in the hospital for a *really* long time.

You became particularly close with a woman you worked with, Midge, and eventually decided to introduce us. I adored her immediately. The three of us went out to an all-night diner one night, and I mentioned something I'd been wanting to try—infusing vodka with different things—if I ever got a job and had my own money. You got *furious*. Said it was a stupid idea and a waste of money. Midge interrupted you—something I wasn't really allowed to do—and stood up for me. "If it's *her* money," she said, "she can do whatever she wants with it. It's okay if it ends up being a mistake." Because of that, I thought she was safe. I started confiding in her about the way you treated me. Later, I found out she wasn't safe at all. She told you everything.

We had been living in that shitty apartment for two and a half years, and had been married for about two. Then we moved about a mile down the road, into a much nicer complex—one that a friend from trivia had just moved into. I *loved* that apartment. It had enough space for a dining table, and I threw myself into homemaking: trying new recipes, getting dinner on the table every night. I've never been the best housekeeper (still true), but I tried. Weekly laundry. Vacuuming. Dishes. All that shit. You never once mentioned how hard I was trying. In fact, you told me I was doing *less* than I had before. And you kept hammering home that if it weren't for you, no one else would want me—and I believed you.

We spent a lot of time with Midge and her husband. You two were so affectionate sometimes that *he* would call me crying at night—he had PTSD from Afghanistan—asking if I thought you and Midge were having an affair. And honestly, it was hard to say. Because she was just as affectionate, if not more, with *me*. I didn't know how to read any of it.

I also kept our budget, and we were always barely scraping by—mostly because you cared more about appearances than about food or bills. I remember one time our power got shut off in the summer. Why? Because you spent $300 at a strip club.

It was around then that I learned the word *gaslighting*. I didn't really get it just from reading about it, so I decided to watch the film that gave the term its name—*Gaslight*, the 1944 version. And *I got it*. That film was exactly how you treated me. All the puzzle pieces started clicking into place. I started reading more, talking to friends online about the way you treated me. That's when I started to realize that almost all of our sex since we got married wasn't really consensual.

I think I was the one who brought up divorce first. But you insisted we didn't need to separate. We could work through it. You promised you wouldn't leave me stranded and jobless. You said you wouldn't let me become homeless again. And I believed you.

I had started talking again with my high school sweetheart—Robert—the one who always understood my soul, even if we hadn't been good as a couple. Around the same time, I reconnected with Kat, my best friend since eighth grade, and Jon, a close friend from that era. You had driven a wedge between me and each of them over the years. I don't remember what exactly prompted the reconnections, but I reached out anyway and decided to come home to Tulsa for the 4th of July. I made plans to see all three of them. I even told you I'd probably hook up with Robert if we met—and you said that was fine. You said you didn't care.

Right before I left, I got an offer for what felt like my dream job. I had nailed the interview, and they wanted me to start as soon as I got back from Tulsa.

The trip itself was a breath of air I hadn't realized I'd been holding. I met up with Jon at Soundpony first, to have beers and meet his girlfriend (who, I later learned, is now his wife). It was a beautiful night. Then I saw Kat and her roommate—we talked, watched movies, and made plans for me to stay at their place the next night. That night was the 4th, and I wanted to be home for the fireworks. The next day I met up with Robert. We talked, and as expected, we hooked up. I crashed at Kat's afterward and then made my way back to Austin.

Before I could even tell you about my trip, you said you wanted a divorce.

That's when your behavior got really fucking unacceptable.

We agreed to separate into different bedrooms while I looked for a new place—just until I got paid from the new job and could move out. I took the master bedroom so I could keep the dog and cat with me. It had two doors: one from the hallway and one from the bathroom, which also connected to the hall. I didn't think anything of it at the time.

But that bathroom door? It only locked from the bathroom side. It opened into the bathroom too, so I couldn't even block it with a chair. You promised you'd be respectful.

You fucking weren't.

Every night, I'd wake up to your dick pressed against me. Or inside me. Your hands, your mouth, all over me. I didn't know how to stop you from getting in. So I started drinking the moment I woke up. I was really into sweet tea vodka then—mixing it with sweet tea and bringing a couple bottles to work. Or I'd drink half a soda and top it off with rum or vodka. No one at work ever said a word.

One time, I secretly went to bed with a kitchen knife I'd picked up somewhere, determined to cut you if you tried anything that night. You did. I tried to fight, but you got the knife out of my hand and held it to my neck. My dog, Valentine—truly the best dog in the world—jumped on you, snapping and biting. I had never seen her do so much as growl before that moment. After that night, she wouldn't let you anywhere near me if she was in the room.

We lived close to my job, but I started arranging to stay with friends across town just to avoid being in the same apartment. One night after work, a group of us went to the karaoke bar, like we usually did. I normally managed to keep from drinking too much, but that night, for whatever reason, I didn't. No one wanted to drive me all the way to my friends' place, and I couldn't afford a cab. I checked in with them—they said to feel free to crash somewhere closer, they'd take care of the pets.

For a variety of reasons I don't remember, no one else could put me up. In desperation, I called you. You usually worked overnight shifts, so I hoped you'd be gone and I could just crash on the couch for a few hours before heading to work. But you were off that night. You said it was fine for me to come over, and—again—I believed you when I shouldn't have.

I didn't have Valentine with me this time.

You started ripping my clothes off the second I stepped through the door. You touched me like you actually cared—like you were trying, for once, to do the things I liked, the things you'd always ignored. It almost made it feel okay. Until it wasn't. I said no. Loudly. Repeatedly. It didn't matter. You did what you wanted, then left me drunk and crying on your bed while you played World of Warcraft.

Until you came back and did it again.
And again.
Every hour or two.
All night.

Around 7 a.m., I drove myself home. My friends held me while I cried. They wanted me to file a report, but I didn't have marks or bruises. We were still technically married. Your parents had money. I barely had friends. At least, those were the talking points the cop on the phone fed me to talk me out of filing.

At 9 a.m., I drove back across town and went to work.

Eventually I got my own place. It should have felt like freedom, but instead I got panic attacks. They clamped down on my chest, made it impossible to breathe. Crowds, bands you liked, strange men standing too close—it all set me off. My whole nervous system had been rewired by you.

One day, I saw your fucking car in my apartment complex. You didn't see me—I was crouched behind the mailboxes like prey. I didn't even go back inside. I just got in my car and drove to a friend's house and didn't come back till I could pretend to be calm.

Meanwhile, you called. You texted. You emailed. You found ways to stay in my head. And I couldn't block you, because we were still doing the divorce ourselves, DIY-style, like every other broken thing in our lives. The divorce was final two days before our third anniversary. The judge even made a joke—"Don't you want to wait and make it an even three years?" Like it was a goddamn wedding toast.

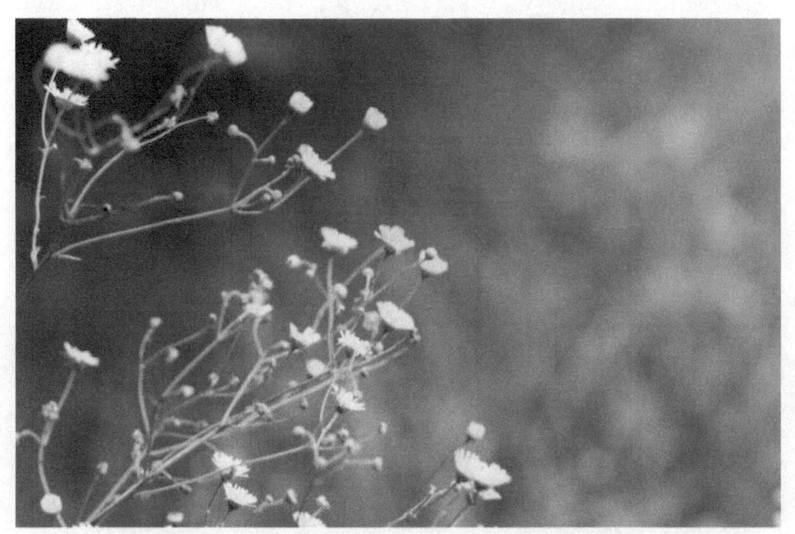

I didn't have Valentine with me this time

Afterward | Unconditional Love

An Essay by Juan De La Cruz

As a child I never understood parenthood. I never knew what they meant by “it’s a different kind of love”. And that perplexing sentence stayed a mystery until my daughter was born. It was a mystery until the moment she stopped crying and looked into my eyes and smiled, then it was clear.

This love is one of no reception needed, it is as present as the sun in the sky, or the water in the ocean. It is a love that lives as she does; nothing was given, or received to give reason for its presence. There was no build up, no nervousness at the beginning. It was there, and it has always been there waiting. A fullness, that no matter what you’ve done seemed to always be just out of reach. The idea that gave reality to hope, giving the appearance of full to what only felt a fraction.

It is said that there are no words, but these are mine , warm, transcendent, pure, unwavering, innocent, and unconditional. This is no love a story, movie, song, or play can fully interpret, for you cannot fully feel the longing of an interpretation of an interpretation. You cannot feel the calm of tiny eyes and knowing you serve them, and a sentence that gives ground to resistance, now fills your heart with an eternal will.

Where I draw confusion is on those who walk away from this love. My knowledge falters in understanding how you could deny this happiness; even more so how you could hurt this, ridicule this, damn this, or even renounce this. A love like this does not deserve to be turned away from for mere disagreement, or the division of perspective of life. These children are a part of you, living and breathing, and an undeniable miracle and yet they treat them as something easily obtainable or replaceable.

This is where I see the space to build a stronger foundation in our faculties of belief. Because what does it say about our society, when this love is tainted or taken for granted and it stands as a staple in households and fades into normality of the walls, and fabric of our families.

To have a family, and to fill it with unconditional love is the greatest gift you can give yourself and the ones you love, to be present, to be their home. This love does not need to be explained, or convinced; that is why no one tries. No one tries to convince one to wake up in the morning, or explain what it is like to live. For as life is meant to be lived this love is meant to be felt. Because words do not do it justice.

Now I understand what it means: “a different kind of love”. And I know how to cherish it; so I will tend to it as a gardener tends to their lilies, and their roses. For I know each day I do, I give love to more buds that blossom and share in this sun's light. And in doing so I hope in time these bushes bring abundance to the land, so that our children’s children know how to love the flowers that come from the seeds we leave behind.

About the Contributors

H.V. Patterson (she/her)

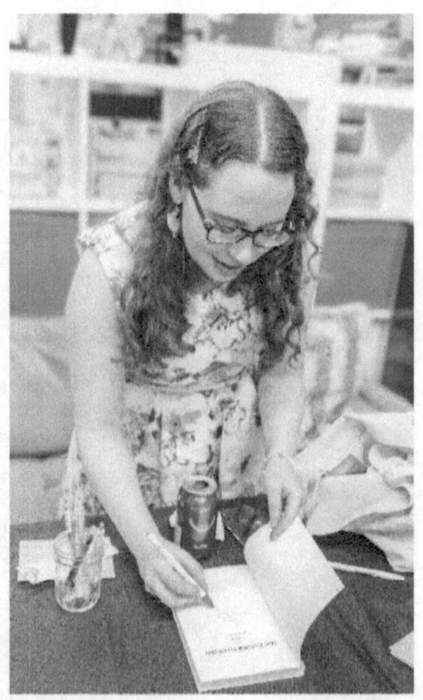

H.V. Patterson (she/her) lives in Oklahoma and writes speculative fiction, poetry, and plays. She loves cooking and baking, but finds the constant battle against dust and general household disorder aggravating. Recent publications include *Haven Speculative, Small Wonders, Flash Fiction Online,* and *Best Horror of the Year.* She's a cofounder of *Horns and Rattles Press*, and you can find her on Bluesky @hvpatterson and on Instagram @hvpattersonwriter, or at hvpatterson.com

Mariah Gonzales (she/they)

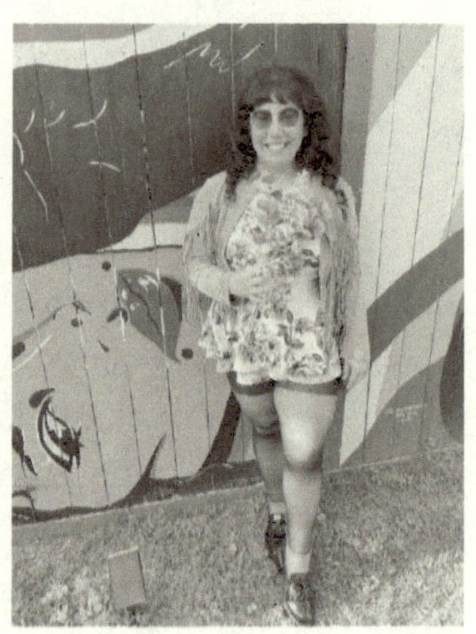

Mariah Gonzales is a poet, violinist, and video editor based in Oklahoma. Her work explores grief, girlhood, and resistance. She studied film at the University of Tulsa and spends her time writing, playing violin in a community orchestra, and organizing with local mutual aid groups. She believes in the power of art to build community and keep memories alive.

Juan De La Cruz (he/him)

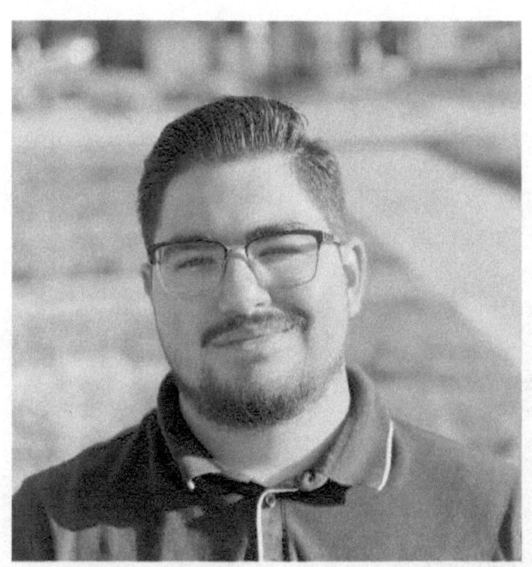

Electrician by day and poet by night. Juan spends his time when not working or being a father, studying philosophy, the written word, going to the gym, or planning his next performance for an open mic. He is a firm believer in the power of will and justice for oneself or others and uses his writing as a vehicle for introspective discovery and a lens to look into the depth of the human experience. He credits all his inspiration to his wonderful fiancé and their daughter as well as his upbringing in Tulsa as a mixed Latino.

Jes McCutchen (she/her)

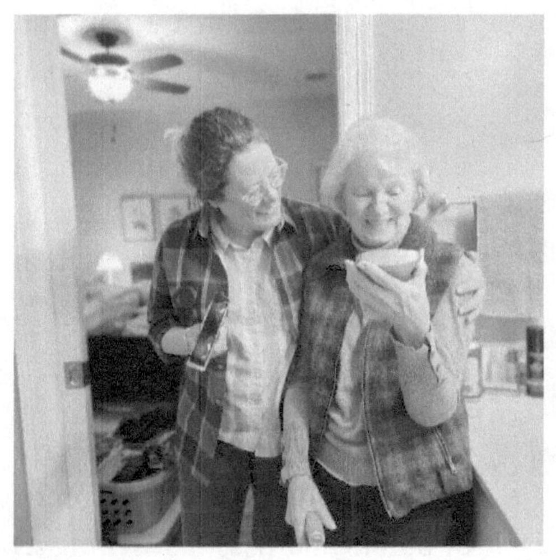

Jes McCutchen (she/her/hers) lives in Tulsa with her partner Marshall, and their son. As well as one stinky weenie dog named Fable Rose. When not writing poetry, she writes queer YA science fiction and fantasy novels that always have happy endings, and makes art. She struggled with postpartum depression and anxiety, and is currently medicated. You can find more information and contact her at jesmccutchenwrites.com.

KJ Shephard (he/him)

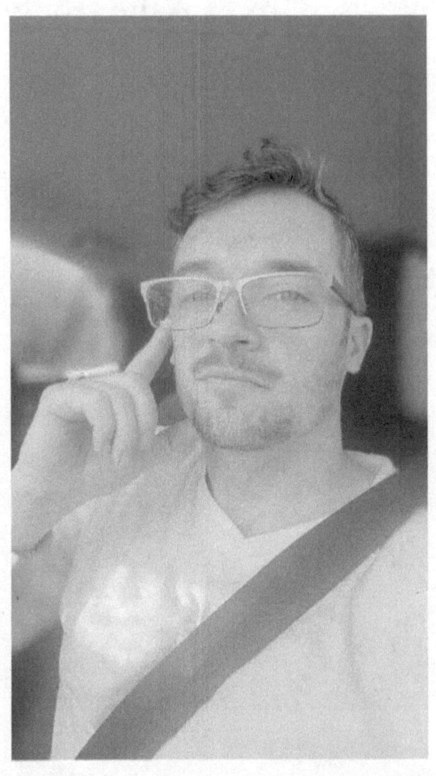

Kyle grew up in Texas, mostly, and is, unfortunately, still there! He currently resides in San Marcos with his teenage kiddo, Harper, and their cat called Potato. If he's not writing, he's gardening, playing Smash Bros, building Lego, painting or drawing, cooking, baking, pickling, (mustarding?), jamming, jellying, and way too many other side projects. He's most active on TikTok as KyleDoesWords. He just recently started wearing hats and is pretty stoked about it tbh.

Ashe (they/them)

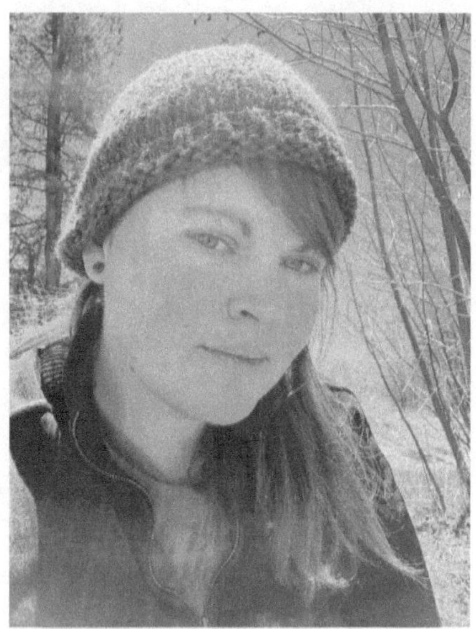

Ashe is a bandrui poet who emphasizes life with lyric both on and off the page. When not adventuring, they enjoy the ride as a parent, a friend and a pirate. Ahoy maties!

Tina Wall (she/her)

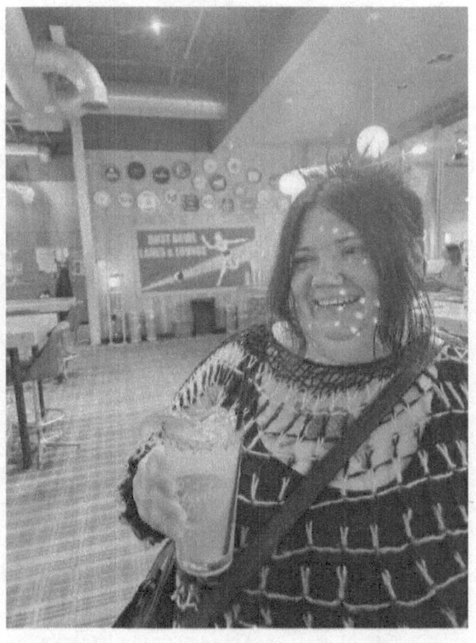

Tina Wall (she/her) exists in this world like many of us do. She was born here in Tulsa, grew up in Sand Springs. She went away for her 20s and 30s, but now she's back to make her 40s EVERYONE'S problem. She is an artist and chaos gremlin who works with data when she needs to pay rent or buy pet food. She lives with her wonderfully understanding spouse, two dogs, a cat, and whatever the cat keeps hunting at night.

M. Torres (she/her)

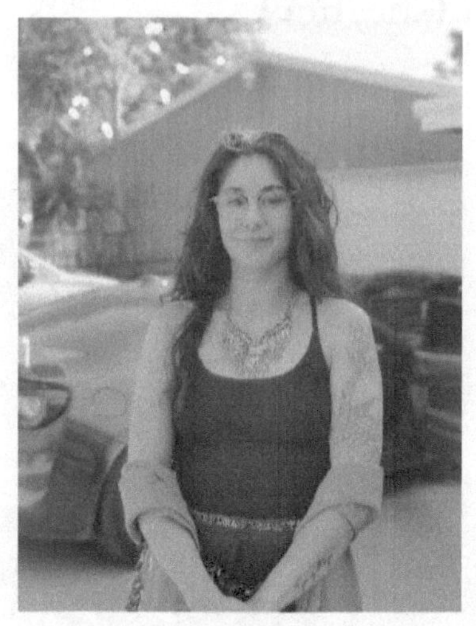

M. Torres is a professional photographer, consultant, and entrepreneur based in Tulsa, Oklahoma and available for travel. As the founder of **Torres Fine Art Photography Studios** and **Torres & Co.**, she merges creative direction with strategic consulting to help small businesses clarify their brand, refine workflows, and grow sustainably. A registered photographer since 2014, Megan's fine art and commercial work has been featured in exhibitions and publications throughout the years, known for its emotive storytelling and attention to detail. She also serves as director of a nonprofit Latin American dance group *(Tierra Mestiza)*, reflecting her deep commitment to cultural preservation and community impact. Balancing her roles as an artist, consultant, and independent mother, Megan leads with purpose, authenticity, and an unwavering dedication to empowering others through art and enterprise.

Sapira Cheuk (she/her)

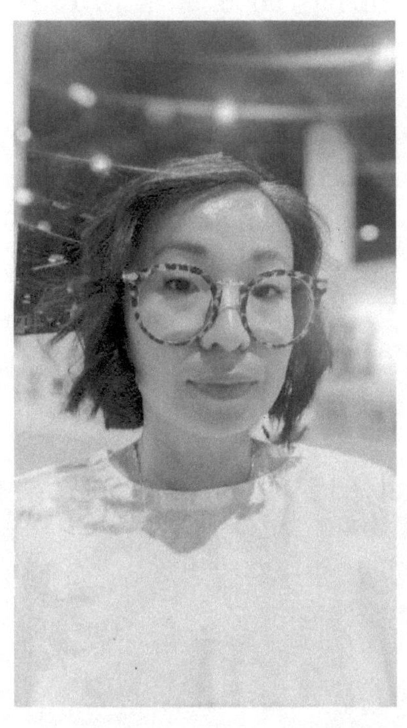

Sapira Cheuk (she/her) is an ink painter and installation artist. Born in Hong Kong and based in Las Vegas, NV. Cheuk's work often utilizes a blend of sumi and india ink, symbolizing the mixture of her identities. Cheuk has exhibited in numerous exhibitions, including at the Institute of Contemporary Art Los Angeles, the Royal Society of Art, London, UK, Center for Contemporary Art Texas, Pablo Center for the Arts, Eau, Masur Museum, and Yellowstone Art Museum. Cheuk works for the Nevada Arts Council, and teaches at the College of Southern Nevada. She serves as the Chair of City of Las Vegas Art Commissioner and as a grant panelist for the National Endowment for the Arts. She received her BA at the University of California, Riverside, and MFA from California State University, San Bernardino.

Acknowledgements

Thank you to the flourishing literary community in Tulsa that gets to our roots and digs them up. Thank you to everyone who contributed to this collection for your patience, your flexibility, your enthusiasm and your trust in me to create this anthology. Your words matter, and I'm honored to be part of getting them out into the world. And as always, to Marshall and G. I love you both so much. - *Jes*

Dedicated to my mother, Debra Carol Gonzales. Thank you for loving me beyond this life. I'm still figuring it out without you. - *Mariah*

Eternal thanks to my spouse Brian for always supporting me. Additional thanks to the many therapists I saw between my first marriage and this one. - *Tina*

To my fiancé, our daughter and my mom. The women who taught me to be loving, caring and compassionate. - *Juan*

With heartfelt gratitude, I thank the communities and collaborators who continue to inspire my work—especially those who trust me to tell their stories through imagery and those who choose to have my work help tell their stories *(especially looking at you Jes)*. To my fellow artists, clients, the Tulsa creative community, and my creative community across the country - your support fuels my passion. And to save the best for last to my wild child Javier, my best friends *(for putting up with us),* and mentors for grounding me in purpose and pushing me to grow, with my utmost respect I thank you. - *Megan*

I'd like to thank the grandmothers of the land, the land herself and the sisters of the sea. - *Ashe*

There is no way I'd be where I am today without those I love most. Harper is always there to talk about any random story idea I have. My best friend, Steph, is much the same, and her support means more than the world to me; I've never loved anyone in this life more than her, and will be hard pressed to find a more genuine human being. My mom is my biggest fan and supporter and I love her dearly. And lastly, Jes McCutchen, without whom I wouldn't have gotten any of these pieces in on time!!! - *Kyle*

Big thanks to my amazing spouse, loving family, and my ride or die pals. I couldn't have done it without you! - *Sapira*

I'm so thankful for all the support I've received from writers near and far, especially Whitty Writers. Thank you to my lovely husband, my best friend and biggest supporter. Thank you to my amazing mother, Kate Eleanor, who is my best, first reader--and who collaborated with me on two of these poems. Thank you to Jes for inviting me to contribute to this project and for putting everything together! - *H.V.*

www.ingramcontent.com/pod-product-compliance
Lightning Source LLC
LaVergne TN
LVHW090531110826
845146LV00003B/1063

* 9 7 9 8 9 8 5 9 4 8 6 8 4 *